Har~~~~ ~~~~~
to CEVNI

© RYA
First published 2016
Reprinted March 2017
Reprinted June 2018
Reprinted August 2019
The Royal Yachting Association
RYA House, Ensign Way,
Hamble, Southampton,
Hampshire SO31 4YA

Tel: 02380 604 100

Web: www.rya.org.uk
Follow us on Twitter @RYAPublications
or on YouTube

We welcome feedback on our
publications at
publications@rya.org.uk

You can check content updates
for RYA publications at
www.rya.org.uk/go/bookschangelog

ISBN 978-1-910017104
RYA Order Code G106

Note: While all reasonable care has been taken in
the preparation of this book, the publisher takes no
responsibility for the use of the methods or products or
contracts described in this book.

Cover design: Jude Williams
Cover photographs: Rob & Sue Brailey;
charterbarge.com
Illustration credits: Illustrations on pages 24–25, 27,
30–45 taken from CEVNI European Code for Inland
Waterways (Fifth revised edition), by United Nations
Economic Commission for Europe Inland Transport
Committee Working Party on Inland Water Transport,
© 2015 United Nations. Reprinted with the permission
of the United Nations.
Acknowledgements: Rob Gibson; Roy May
Typeset: Jude Williams
Proofreading: Rob Melotti
Printed in China through World Print

Contents

Many European countries require the skipper of a pleasure craft to be able to provide evidence of his or her competence. Experiences differ greatly. Inconsistency from province to province and port to port means many boaters are never asked to provide evidence of their competence abroad. However, those that are asked and do not have a suitable document can find themselves in an uncomfortable situation. This is where an ICC can prove to be useful.

The ICC (or, to give it its full title, International Certificate for Operators of Pleasure Craft) is a certificate which is intended to provide evidence of competence when requested by officials in foreign countries. It is sometimes known as the International Certificate of Competence.

It is issued under the United Nations Economic Commission for Europe (UNECE) Inland Transport Committee Working Party on Inland Water Transport Resolution 40. It is this resolution which details how and to whom the ICC may be issued, the syllabus requirements, the layout of the certificate, and the countries which have notified the UNECE Secretariat that they have accepted the resolution. Resolution 40 requires that applicants for the ICC prove that they have sufficient knowledge and ability to safely operate a pleasure craft. This can be done by presenting a recognised national certificate issued by the country which is issuing the ICC. Alternatively, the resolution makes provision for boaters to pass an examination.

The UK ICC issued by the RYA has five categories: inland waters, coastal waters, power, sail (including auxiliary engine), and personal watercraft. When an ICC is issued, only the categories for which competence has been demonstrated will be validated. Your ICC will need to be valid for both the type of boat and the type of waters in which you intend boating.

Resolution 40 requires that candidates for coastal waters have knowledge of the International Regulations for Preventing Collisions at Sea (COLREGS), and candidates applying for an ICC with the inland category validated have sufficient knowledge of the traffic regulations applicable on inland waters, in particular Code Européen des Voies de Navigation Intérieure (CEVNI). Every candidate wishing to have the inland category validated on their ICC must therefore first pass the ICC CEVNI test.

CEVNI is the code governing navigation on the interconnected European inland waterways and is the basis of many of the various countries' own regulations.

Signs, rules, and procedures for navigating many of the European inland waterways are all included within CEVNI and, in the same way as pleasure craft on coastal waters are expected to abide by the COLREGS, pleasure craft on many of the inland waterways of Europe, which in places are heavily utilised by commercial traffic, are expected to know and follow the applicable traffic regulations, in particular CEVNI.

CEVNI is not covered in any of the RYA's courses, even those specific to inland waterways, as these regulations are not in use in the UK. It is therefore necessary to have a separate theory test on the CEVNI regulations.

There is, however, no separate CEVNI certificate or CEVNI endorsement. Passing the CEVNI test simply allows the inland category on your ICC to be validated, thereby indicating that you have demonstrated knowledge of the CEVNI regulations as required by the resolution.

All candidates requiring the inland category validated must pass the ICC CEVNI test, irrespective of whether the CEVNI regulations are used in the country or on the river, lake or canal where they intend to go boating.

For more information on CEVNI and to gain a greater understanding of its wider context, please visit **https://www2.unece.org/wiki/display/TransportSustainableCEVNIv5/CEVNI+-+Revision+5.** This defines terms and procedures in greater detail.

The RYA ICC CEVNI test is a multiple-choice paper. Costs for the CEVNI test will vary between organisations (RYA recognised training centres and RYA affiliated clubs). There are two options:

- Take the test in person at an RYA recognised training centre or an affiliated club authorised to carry out the test; or

- Many RYA recognised training centres or affiliated clubs authorised to carry out the test can provide you with access to take the test online remotely from home or anywhere in the world.

In addition to passing the CEVNI test, for an ICC to be issued you must present a qualifying RYA practical course completion certificate, or pass an ICC assessment at an RYA recognised training centre and be eligible to be issued with an ICC.

To find out more about the ICC CEVNI test, please visit:
http://www.rya.org.uk/infoadvice/boatingabroad/icc/Pages/cevnitest.aspx

For further information on the ICC, please visit:
http://www.rya.org.uk/infoadvice/boatingabroad/icc/Pages/ICC.aspx

The Code Européen des Voies de Navigation Intérieure is a resolution of the United Nations Economic Commission for Europe Inland Transport Committee. The resolution is under constant review by the Working Party on Inland Water Transport. The fifth revision of CEVNI was published in the summer of 2015. In order to bring them into force, the rules are adopted by national governments and the four River Commissions into the regulations that apply for their area of authority.

The main European international rivers are managed by specially established inter-Governmental River Commissions entrusted with setting technical and legal standards for their respective river networks. In each country, as in the UK, there may be one or more navigation authorities responsible for implementing their rules within their jurisdiction.

It takes time for the changes to be made to the national, local, and River Commission regulations which bring CEVNI into force. While this book is based on the fifth revision of CEVNI, the rules in force may be based on a previous version. However, the rules in force may not exactly match the relevant revision of CEVNI, as some elements of CEVNI may not be appropriate for the local conditions and there is scope for the implementing navigation authority to alter the rules to suit.

It is the rules in force which will indicate the area in which the rules apply, and which, if you are coming from the sea, will indicate where you change over from adhering to the COLREGs. However, if you are seeing CEVNI signage it will be a good indicator that you are on an inland waterway.

The rules in force may include a requirement to carry a copy of those rules on board. In most cases the rules are not published in English, but that neither negates the requirement to carry them nor provides an excuse for not being aware of your obligations.

There may also be inland waters where the local rules are not based on the CEVNI resolution and a completely different set of rules may be in force.

Within waterways with current, the right bank is on the right of you as you look downstream. In areas where there is no current, such as lakes, broad waterways or canals, the right- and left-hand sides are determined by the competent authority.

Red channel markers relate to the right bank, and green channel markers relate to the left bank, meaning that, should you enter the waterway from the sea, the buoyage would remain constant.

A – PROHIBITORY SIGNS

Usually red and white, often with a red diagonal stripe. These designate actions that you must not take.

B – MANDATORY SIGNS

Square or rectangular, red and white, usually with a red border, or black and yellow lights. These signs must be obeyed.

C – RESTRICTIVE SIGNS

Square with red borders detailing physical restrictions or limitations.

D – RECOMMENDATORY SIGNS

Yellow/green, green and white, or white and blue signs recommending the best way to proceed.

E – INFORMATIVE SIGNS

Blue square or rectangular signs, or green lights/green and white rectangular signs, providing information and indicating permitted activities.

AUXILIARY SIGNS

Red and white squares, or blue and white squares/rectangles with additional information given on them.

A.1 No entry (general sign)

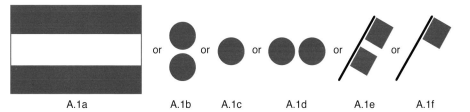

A.1a   A.1b   A.1c   A.1d   A.1e   A.1f

Two boards, two lights or two flags, one above the other, indicate a prolonged prohibition.

A.1.1 Sections closed
to use, no entry
except for
non-motorized
Small Craft.

A.2 No overtaking.

A.3 No overtaking of
convoys by convoys.

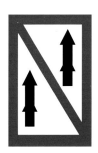

A.4 No passing
or overtaking.

A.4.1 No passing or
overtaking of
convoys by
convoys.

A.5 No berthing on the
side of the waterway
on which the sign
is placed (i.e. no
anchoring or
making fast to
the bank).

Prohibitory Signs

A.5.1 No berthing on the stretch of water whose breadth, measured from the sign, is shown in metres on the sign.

A.6 No anchoring or trailing of anchors, cables or chains on the side of the waterway on which the sign is placed.

A.7 No making fast to the bank on the side of the waterway on which the sign is placed.

A.8 No turning.

A.9 Do not create wash likely to cause damage.

A.9a

or

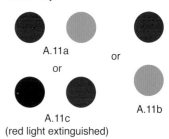

A.9b

A.10 No passing outside the area marked (in openings of bridges or weirs).

A.11 Entry prohibited, but prepare to get under way.

A.11a

or

or

A.11c
(red light extinguished)

A.11b

A.12 Motorized craft prohibited.

A.13 Sports or pleasure craft prohibited.

A.14 Water skiing
prohibited.

A.15 Sailing vessels
prohibited.

A.16 All craft other than
motorized vessels
or sailing craft
prohibited.

A.17 Use of sailboards
prohibited.

A.18 End of zone
authorized for high
speed navigation
of small sport and
pleasure craft.

A.19 No launching or
beaching of vessels.

A.20 Water bikes
prohibited.

B.1 Proceed in the direction shown by the arrow.

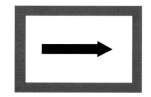

B.2

B.2a Move to the side of the fairway on your port side.

B.2b Move to the side of the fairway on your starboard side.

B.3

B.3a Keep to the side of the fairway on your port side.

B.3b Keep to the side of the fairway on your starboard side.

B.4

B.4a Cross fairway to port.

B.4b Cross fairway to starboard.

B.5 Stop as prescribed in the Regulations.

B.6 Do not exceed the speed indicated (in km/h).

B.7 Give a sound signal.

B.8 Keep a particularly sharp lookout.

B.9 Do not enter or cross the main waterway until certain that this will not oblige vessels proceeding on it to change their course or speed.

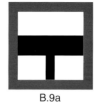

B.9a

B.9b

B.10 Vessels proceeding on the main waterway must, if necessary, change course and speed to allow vessels to leave harbours or tributary waterways.

B.11

B.11a Obligation to enter into a radiotelephone link.

B.11b Obligation to enter into a radiotelephone link on the channel as indicated on the board.

C.1 Depth of water limited.

C.1a

C.1b

C.2 Headroom limited.

C.2a

C.2b

C.3 Width of passage or channel limited.

C.3a

C.3b

C.4 There are restrictions on navigation: see the information plate below the sign.

C.5 The channel lies at a distance from the right (left) bank; the figure shown on the sign indicates the distance in metres, measured from the sign, to which vessels should keep.

D.1 Recommended opening.

(a) In both directions   or

          D.1a   D.1b

(b) Only in the direction
    indicated (passage in   or   or
    the opposite direction
    prohibited)

          D.1c   D.1d   D.1e   D.1f

D.2 You are recommended to keep within the area indicated
    (in openings of bridges or weirs).

   or

          D.2a   D.2b

D.3 You are recommended to proceed:

   or

          D.3a   D.3b
                                  From white light
                                  to isophase.

E.1 Entry permitted (general sign).

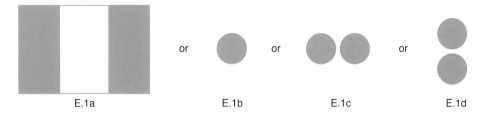

E.1a   E.1b   E.1c   E.1d

E.2 Overhead cable crossing.

E.3 Weir.

E.4a Ferry-boat not moving independently (e.g. a chain ferry).

E.4b Ferry-boat moving independently.

E.5 Berthing (i.e. anchoring or making fast to the bank) permitted on the side of the waterway on which the sign is placed.

E.5.1 Berthing permitted on the stretch of water of the breadth measured from, and shown on the board in metres.

E.5.2 Berthing permitted on the stretch of water bounded by the two distances measured from, and shown on the board in metres.

E.5.3 Maximum number of vessels permitted to berth abreast on the side of the waterway on which the sign is placed.

E.5.4 Berthing area reserved for pushing-navigation vessels that are not required to carry the marking prescribed in article 3.14 on the side of the waterway on which the sign is placed.

E.5.5 Berthing area reserved for pushing-navigation vessels that are required to carry one blue light or one blue cone under article 3.14, paragraph 1, on the side of the waterway on which the sign is placed.

E.5.6 Berthing area reserved for pushing-navigation vessels that are required to carry two blue lights or two blue cones under article 3.14, paragraph 2, on the side of the waterway on which the sign is placed.

E.5.7 Berthing area reserved for pushing-navigation vessels that are required to carry three blue lights or three blue cones under article 3.14, paragraph 3, on the side of the waterway on which the sign is placed.

E.5.8 Berthing area reserved for vessels other than pushing-navigation vessels that are not required to carry the marking prescribed in article 3.14 on the side of the waterway on which the sign is placed.

E.5.9 Berthing area reserved for vessels other than pushing-navigation vessels that are required to carry one blue light or one blue cone under article 3.14, paragraph 1, on the side of the waterway on which the sign is placed.

E.5.10 Berthing area reserved for vessels other than pushing-navigation vessels that are required to carry two blue lights or two blue cones under article 3.14, paragraph 2, on the side of the waterway on which the sign is placed.

E.5.11 Berthing area reserved for vessels other than pushing-navigation vessels that are required to carry three blue lights or three blue cones under article 3.14, paragraph 3, on the side of the waterway on which the sign is placed.

E.5.12 Berthing area reserved for all vessels that are not required to carry the marking prescribed in article 3.14, on the side of the waterway on which the sign is placed.

E.5.13 Berthing area reserved for all vessels that are required to carry one blue light or one blue cone under article 3.14, paragraph 1, on the side of the waterway on which the sign is placed.

E.5.14 Berthing area reserved for all vessels that are required to carry two blue lights or two blue cones under article 3.14, paragraph 2.

E.5.15 Berthing area reserved for all vessels that are required to carry three blue lights or three blue cones under article 3.14, paragraph 3, on the side of the waterway on which the sign is placed.

E.6 Anchoring (see article 7.03, para. 2) or trailing of anchors, cables or chains permitted on the side of the waterway on which the sign is placed.

E.6.1 Use of spuds permitted.

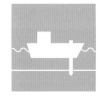

E.7 Making fast to the bank permitted on the side of the waterway on which the sign is placed.

E.7.1 Berthing area reserved for loading and unloading vehicles. (Maximum duration of berthing permitted may be added on an information plate below the board).

E.8 Turning area.

E.9 The waterways being approached are considered to be tributaries of this waterway.

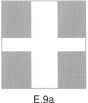

E.9a

E.9b

E.9c

E.10 This waterway is considered to be a tributary of the waterway being approached.

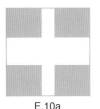

E.10a   E.10b

E.11 End of a prohibition or obligation applying to traffic in one direction only, or end of a restriction.

E.11a

E.11b

E.12 Advance signals: one or two white lights.

E.12a

E.12b

E.12c

E.12d

(a) Fixed light(s): Difficulty ahead – stop if the regulations so require.

(b) Isophase light(s): You may proceed.

E.13 Drinking-water supply.

E.14 Telephone.

E.15 Motorized vessels permitted.

E.16 Sports or pleasure craft permitted.

E.17 Water skiing permitted.

E.18 Sailing vessels permitted.

E.19 Craft other than motorized vessels or sailing craft permitted.

E.20 Use of sailboards permitted.

E.21 Zone authorized for high speed navigation of small sport and pleasure craft.

E.22 Launching or beaching of Small Craft permitted.

E.23 Possibility of obtaining nautical information by radio-telephone on the channel indicated.

E.24 Water bikes permitted.

E.25 Electrical power supply point.

E.26 Winter harbour.

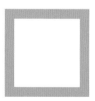

E.26.1 Maximum number of vessels permitted to berth in winter harbour.

E.27 Winter shelter.

E.27.1 Maximum number of vessels permitted to berth in winter shelter. Maximum number of vessels permitted to berth abreast. Maximum number of rows of vessels which are berthed abreast.

The main signs (see section I) may be supplemented by the following auxiliary signs:

A. Panels showing the distance at which the regulation applies or the special feature indicated by the main sign is to be found

Note: The panels are placed above the main sign.

Examples:

In 1,000m, stop.

In 1,500m, ferry boat not moving independently.

B. Additional luminous signal

Luminous white arrow combined with certain lights, with the following meanings:

Examples:

(a) With green light Example: Permission to enter the basin to which the arrow is pointing.

(b) With red light Example: No entry to the basin to which the arrow is pointing.

C. Pointers showing the direction of the section to which the main sign applies

Note: The pointers need not necessarily be white and may be placed beside or below the main sign.
Examples:

Berthing permitted.

Berthing prohibited (over a distance of 1,000m).

D. Panels giving explanations or additional information

Note: These panels are placed below the main sign.

Examples:

DOUANE
Stop for Customs.

Give one long blast.

Buoyage of Fairway Limits in the Waterway

Right-hand side of the fairway

1.A Buoy with light.

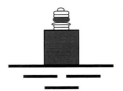

1.B Buoy without light.

1.C Float with a topmark.

1.D Spar.

Left-hand side of the fairway

2.A Buoy with light.

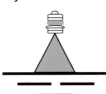

2.B Buoy without light.

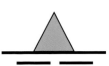

2.C Float with a topmark.

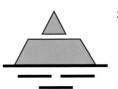

2.D Spar.

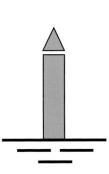

Bifurcation of the fairway

3.A Buoy with light.

3.B Buoy without light.

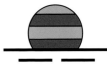

3.C Float with a topmark.   3.D Spar.

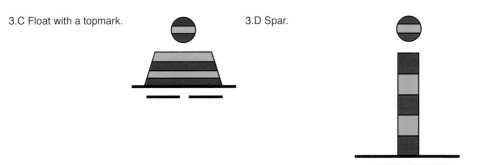

Where necessary, a red cylindrical topmark or green conical topmark placed above the bifurcation mark indicates on which side it is preferable to pass (main fairway).

The mark shall then bear a rhythmic red light or a rhythmic green light, as appropriate.

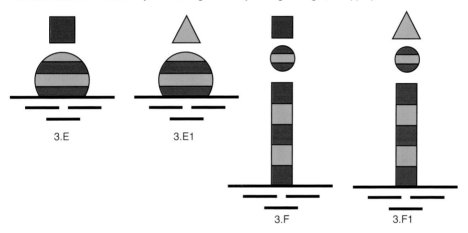

3.E   3.E1   3.F   3.F1

Marks on Land Indicating the Position of the Fairway

Marks on land indicating the position of the fairway in relation to the banks

These marks indicate the position of the fairway in relation to the bank and, together with the buoyage of the waterway, mark the fairway at points where it approaches a bank; they also serve as landmarks.

Channel near the right bank

4.A With light.

4.B Without light.

Channel near the left bank

5.A With light.

5.B Without light.

Use of marks

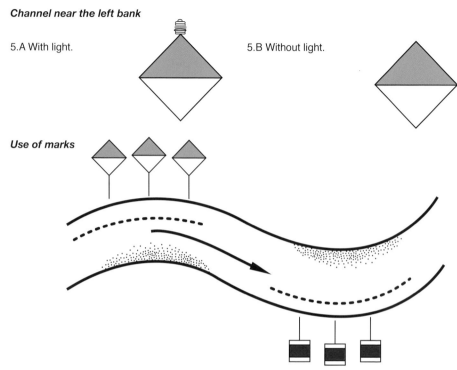

Marking of Cross-overs

These marks indicate at what point the fairway passes from one bank to another and also give the axis of this cross-over.

Right bank

4.C With light.

4.D Without light.

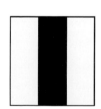

Left bank

5.C With light.

5.D Without light.

Use of Marks

Mere indication of cross-over:

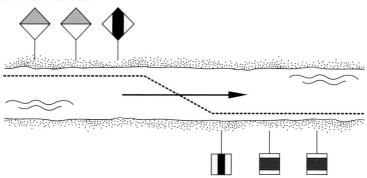

Indication of the axis of a long cross-over:

Two identical signs placed one behind the other on the same bank, the first sign positioned lower than the second one, forming an alignment marking the axis of a long cross-over.

Lights (if any): yellow (the forward light and rearward light generally having the same rhythm; however, the rearward light may be a fixed light).

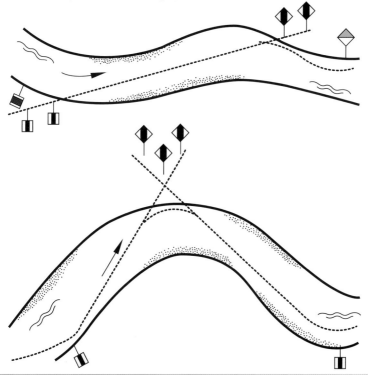

Buoyage and Marking of Danger Points and Obstacles

Fixed marks

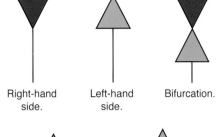

Right-hand side. Left-hand side. Bifurcation.

Buoys

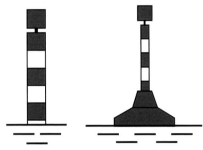

Right-hand side.

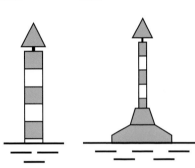

Left-hand side.

Other Marking of Danger Points and Obstacles in the Waterway

Passage permitted on the clear side without reducing speed

BY NIGHT		BY DAY	
Obstructed Side		*Obstructed Side*	
One red light	●	No entry sign	▬
		or	
		One red ball	●
Clear Side		*Clear Side*	
Two green lights one above the other	○ ○	Entry permitted	▮▮
		or	
		Two green bicones one above the other	◇ ◇

Passage permitted on the clear side at reduced speed (avoid creating wash)

BY NIGHT		BY DAY	
Obstructed Side		*Obstructed Side*	
One red light	●	One red flag or red board	■
Clear Side		*Clear Side*	
One red light above one white light	● ○	One red flag or board above one white flag or board	▬

Additional Marking for Navigation by Radar

Marking of bridge piers (where applicable)

Yellow floats with radar reflector (placed upstream and downstream from piers).

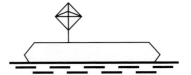

Pole with radar reflector placed upstream and downstream from bridge piers.

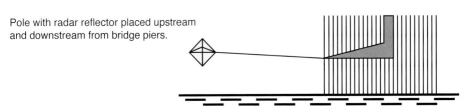

Marking of overhead cables (where applicable)

Radar reflectors secured to the overhead cable (giving a radar image of a series of points to identify the overhead cable).

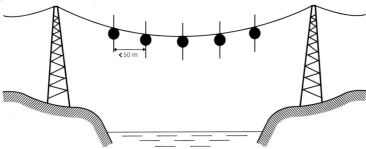

Radar reflectors placed on yellow floats arranged in pairs near each bank (each pair giving a radar image of two points side by side to identify the overhead cable).

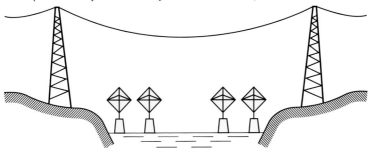

Additional Buoyage and Marking of Lakes and Broad Waterways

Cardinal marks

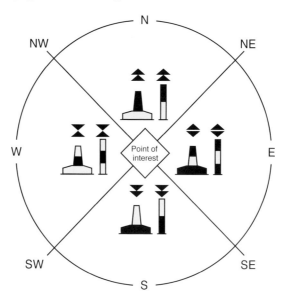

Isolated danger marks

An isolated danger mark is a mark erected on, or moored above an isolated danger which has safe water all around it.

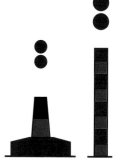

Marking of the axis of a channel, the middle of a channel or a landfall

Safe-water marks.

There are two categories of vessel on the European inland waterways:

Small Craft: Any vessel with a hull less than 20m long without rudder or bowsprit, except vessels built or equipped to tow, push or propel vessels other than Small Craft in side-by-side formation and except craft authorised to carry more than 12 passengers, ferry boats and pushed barges.

Normal Vessels: Any other vessel, commercial or leisure.

Small Craft must give absolute priority to all other craft.

The rules state that 'Small Craft in relation to vessels other than Small Craft shall leave them enough room to hold their course and to manoeuvre. They may not require that such vessels give them way.' They should navigate within 10 metres of the edge of the channel on their right-hand side when in channels or prescribed traffic lanes.

  • Motorised Small Craft give way to non-motorised and sailing Small Craft.

  • Non-motorised Small Craft give way to Small Craft sailing.

The 'stand-on' vessel is expected to keep a steady course, although on inland waters it must be prepared to manoeuvre to avoid a collision.

This section contains a selection of the most common navigation lights and is not exhaustive. Please consult the CEVNI European Code for Inland Waterways (Annex 3) for the full list.

All vessels under way on the waterways after dark must carry running lights comprising a white stern light, green starboard light and red port light. These side lights must be at the same height and unable to be seen from the opposite side. Motorised vessels must also carry a white masthead light of not less than 5m (4m for a vessel of less than 40m length).

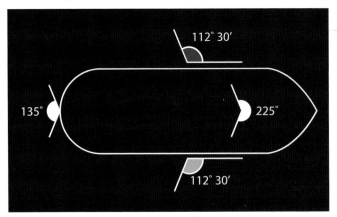

The horizontal arc along which the masthead light, the side lights and the stern light are visible.

Explanation of Symbols

A. Fixed light visible from all directions (a light projecting an uninterrupted beam throughout a horizontal arc of 360°).

B. Fixed light visible over a limited horizontal arc. A light which is invisible to the observer is marked by a dot in the centre.

C. Scintillating light.

D. Optional light.

E. Board or flag.

F. Pennant.

G. Ball.

H. Cylinder.

I. Cone.

J. Bicone.

K. Radar reflector.

Marking When Under Way

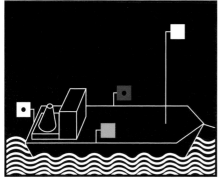

Motorized vessels proceeding alone.

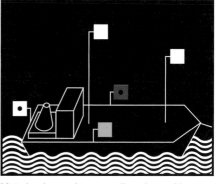

Motorized vessels proceeding alone with a second masthead light. Compulsory for vessels more than 110 m long.

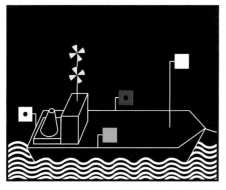

High-speed motorized vessel proceeding alone.

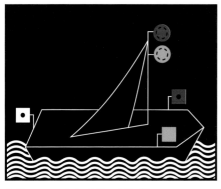

Sailing vessels (not Small Craft).

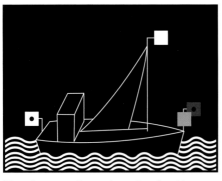 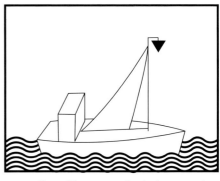

Vessels proceeding under sail and making use at the same time of its own mechanical means of propulsion.

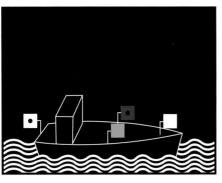 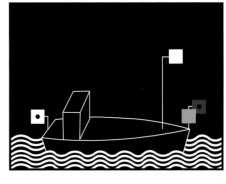

Motorized Small Craft proceeding alone.

Motorized Small Craft proceeding alone with side lights side by side or in the same lamp at or near the bow.

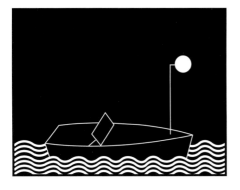 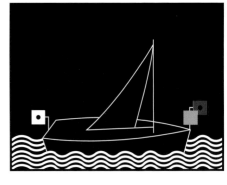

Motorized Small Craft less than 7m long proceeding alone.

Small sailing craft.

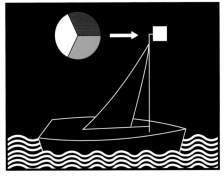

Small sailing craft, with side lights and a stern
light in the same lamp near the top of the mast.

Vessels carrying hazardous substances can be identified by one, two or three blue lights (by night)
or downwards-pointing cones (by day).

One cone/light = flammable material

Two cones/lights = health hazard

Three cones/lights = explosive material

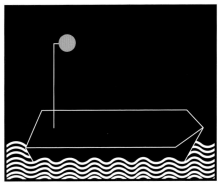
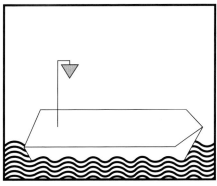

Additional marking for vessels carrying out certain transport operations involving dangerous
substances: flammable.

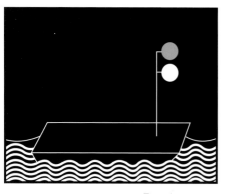
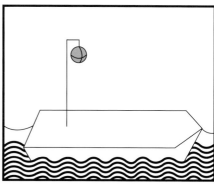

Ferry-boats not moving independently.

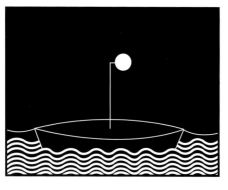

Leading boat or float of a longitudinal-cable ferry-boat.

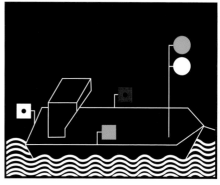

Ferry-boats moving independently.

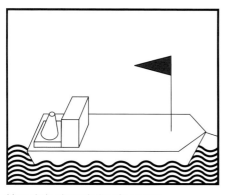

Vessels having priority of passage.

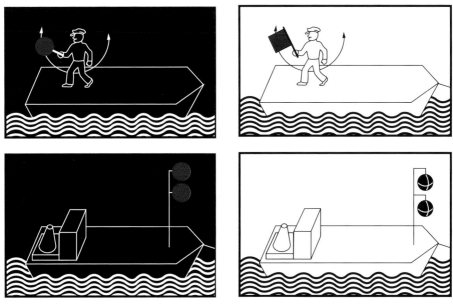

Additional marking for vessels unable to manoeuvre.

Towing

The light characteristics in this section relate to Normal Vessels, not Small Craft. However, it is important to understand how a towed or pushed convoy is controlled and managed to be able to make an informed assessment of the situation. There can be multiple vessels involved, all with specific light and shape characteristics, which can be complex.

There are lead pushing vessels and auxiliaries. The lead vessel or the pushing vessel provides the power to move the convoy, but at various points it may be accompanied and assisted by one or more auxiliary vessels. Therefore, convoys may well change depending on the situation.

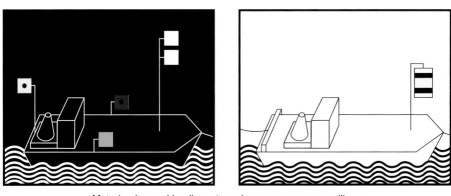

Motorized vessel leading a towed convoy or as an auxiliary.

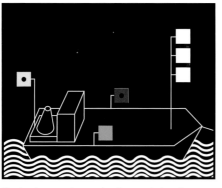 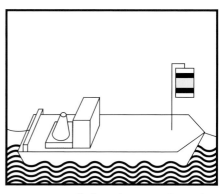

Each of several motorized vessels leading a towed convoy or as auxiliaries, when several vessels are proceeding side by side.

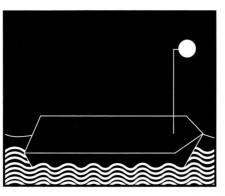 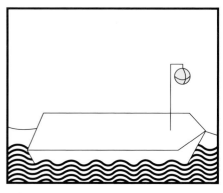

Towed vessels.

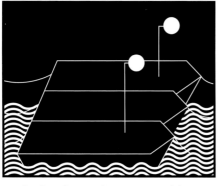 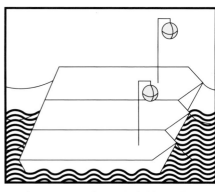

Section of a towed convoy comprising a row of more than two vessels coupled side by side.

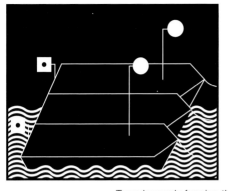
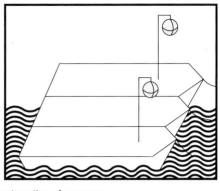

Towed vessels forming the last section of a convoy.

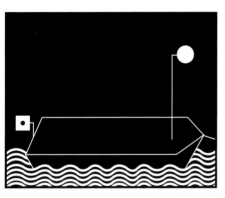
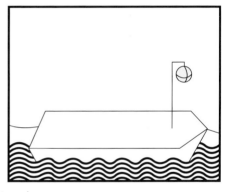

Last section of a towed convoy.

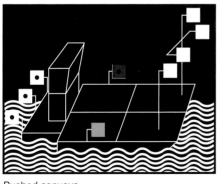
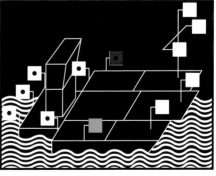

Pushed convoys.

Pushed convoys, when more than two vessels other than the pusher are visible from astern over the full width.

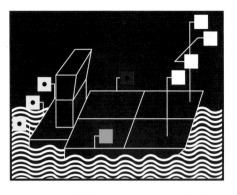 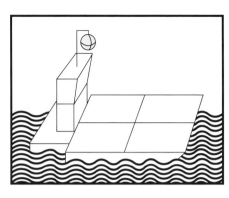

Pushed convoys preceded by one or more auxiliary motorized vessels.

Marking When Stationary

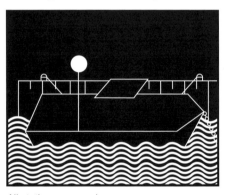

All stationary vessels.

 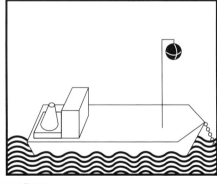

Vessels stationary offshore.

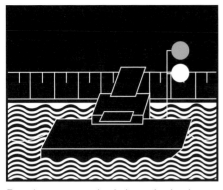

Ferry-boats not moving independently when made fast at their landing stage.

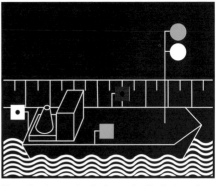

Ferry-boats moving independently, but made fast at their landing stage.

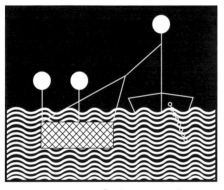

Stationary vessels engaged in fishing with nets or poles.

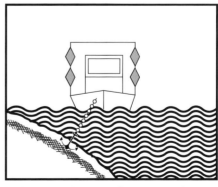

Floating equipment at work and stationary vessels carrying out work or sounding or measuring operations; fairway clear on both sides.

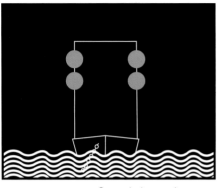 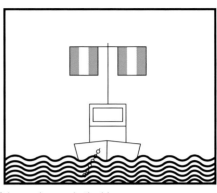

Grounded or sunken vessels; fairway clear on both sides.

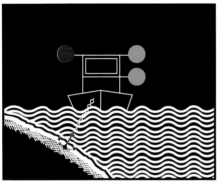 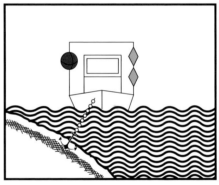

Floating equipment at work and stationary vessels carrying out work or sounding or measuring operations; fairway clear on one side.

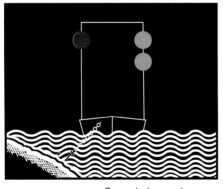 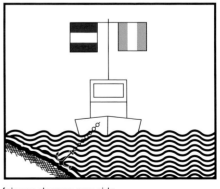

Grounded or sunken vessels; fairway clear on one side.

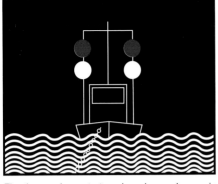 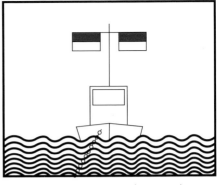

Floating equipment at work and vessels carrying out work or sounding or measuring operations and grounded or sunken vessels; protection against wash; fairway clear on both sides.

 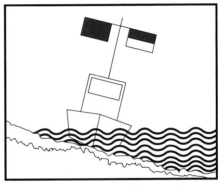

Floating equipment at work and vessels carrying out work or sounding or measuring operations and grounded or sunken vessels; protection against wash; fairway clear on one side.

 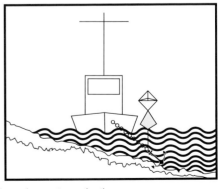

Vessels whose anchors may be a danger to navigation.

Special Marking

 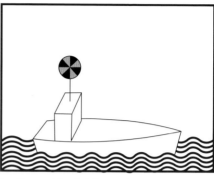

Additional marking for vessels of the supervisory authorities and fire-fighting and rescue services.

 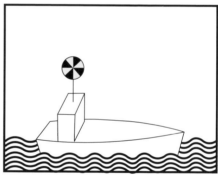

Additional marking for vessels under way carrying out work in the waterway.

 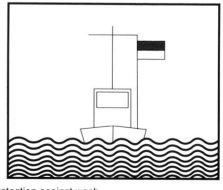

Additional marking for protection against wash.

Distress signals.

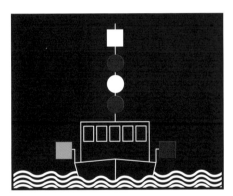 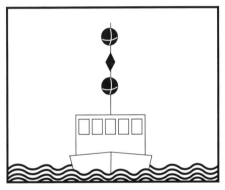

Additional marking for vessels whose ability to manoeuvre is limited.

 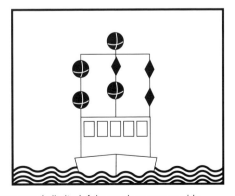

Additional marking for vessels whose ability to manoeuvre is limited; fairway clear on one side.

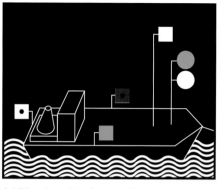 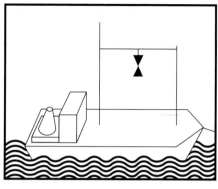

Additional marking for vessels engaged in drawing a trawl or other fishing gear through the water (trawler).

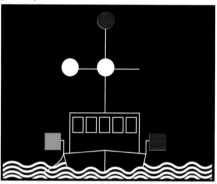 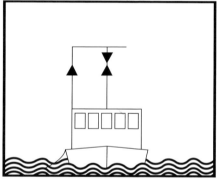

Fishing vessels other than trawlers if the fishing tackle extends more than 150m horizontally from the vessel.

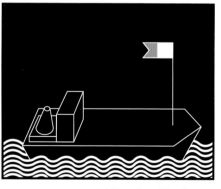 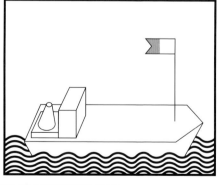

Additional marking for vessels used for underwater diving.

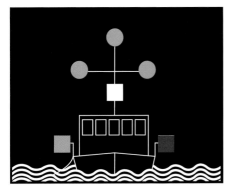 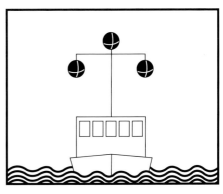

Additional marking for vessels engaged in minesweeping.

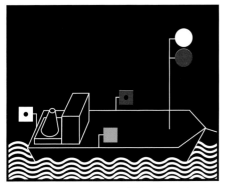 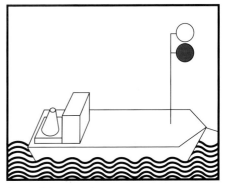

Additional marking for vessels on pilotage service.

Sound Signals

Small Craft give way to Normal Vessels, and there are therefore certain sound signals that they will not use, although helmsmen must still know all of them. The ones that are available to Small Craft are coloured blue in the general signals table. Sound signals other than the ringing of a bell and the three-tone signal shall consist of the emission of one blast or of several successive blasts having the following characteristics:

Short blast: a blast lasting about one second. ▬

Long blast: a blast lasting about four seconds. ▬▬

The interval between two successive blasts shall be about one second except for the signal 'series of very short blasts' which shall comprise a series of not less than six blasts, each lasting about a quarter of a second, separated by a silence of the same duration.

A. General signals

▬	One long blast	Caution
▬	One short blast	I am altering my course to starboard
▬ ▬	Two short blasts	I am altering my course to port
▬ ▬ ▬	Three short blasts	I am going astern
▬ ▬ ▬ ▬	Four short blasts	I am unable to manoeuvre
▬ ▬▬▬ ····	One short blast, one long blast, repeated	Do not approach
···········	Series of very short blasts	Imminent danger of collision
▬▬▬ ▬▬▬ ····	Repeated long blasts	Distress
🔔···· 🔔 🔔···· 🔔	Ringing of bell	Distress

B. Meeting signals

Request to pass on the port side		
▬	One short blast by vessel proceeding upstream	I wish to pass on the port side
▬	One short blast by vessel proceeding downstream	Agreed; pass on the port side
▬ ▬	Two short blasts by vessel proceeding downstream	No; pass on the starboard side
▬ ▬	Two short blasts by vessel proceeding upstream	Agreed; I will pass on the starboard side

Request to pass on the starboard side		
– –	Two short blasts by vessel proceeding upstream	I wish to pass on the starboard side
– –	Two short blasts by vessel proceeding downstream	Agreed; pass on the starboard side
–	One short blast by vessel proceeding downstream	No; pass on the port side
–	One short blast by vessel proceeding upstream	Agreed; I will pass on the port side

C. Overtaking symbols

Request to overtake on the port side		
—— —— – –	Two long blasts followed by two short blasts by overtaking vessel	I wish to overtake on the port side
–	One short blast by vessel to be overtaken	Agreed; overtake on the port side
– –	Two short blasts by vessel to be overtaken	No; overtake on the starboard side
–	One short blast by overtaking vessel	Agreed; I will overtake on the starboard side

Request to overtake on the starboard side		
—— —— –	Two long blasts followed by one blast by overtaking vessel	I wish to overtake on the starboard side
– –	Two short blasts by vessel to be overtaken	Agreed; overtake on the starboard side
–	One short blast by vessel to be overtaken	No; overtake on the port side
– –	Two short blasts by overtaking vessel	Agreed; I will overtake on the port side

Overtaking impossible		
– – – – –	Five short blasts by vessel to be overtaken	I cannot be overtaken

D. Turning signals

—— -	One long blast followed by one short blast	I am going to turn to starboard
—— - -	One long blast followed by two short blasts	I am going to turn to port

E. Harbours and tributary waterways: entering and leaving, followed by crossing the waterway

E.1 Signals on entering and leaving harbours and tributary waterways		
—— —— —— -	Three long blasts followed by one short blast	I am going to starboard
—— —— —— - -	Three long blasts followed by two short blasts	I am going to port

E.2 Signals on crossing after entering the waterway

—— —— ——	Three long blasts	I am going to cross

followed if necessary by:

—— -	One long blast followed by one short blast	I am going to starboard
—— - -	One long blast followed by two short blasts	I am going to port

F. Signals in reduced visibility

(a) Vessels navigating by radar		
	(i) Vessels, other than Small Craft, proceeding downstream	Three-tone signal repeated as often as necessary
—	(ii) Single vessel proceeding upstream	One long blast

(b) Vessels not navigating by radar		
—	(i) Any vessel proceeding alone	One long blast repeated at least once a minute
— - - - -	(ii) Ferry boats not navigating by radar	One long blast followed by four short blasts; repeated at intervals of not more than one minute